Dog had heard that a baby had been born in Bethlehem. 'I'll organise a welcoming party,' he thought. 'The family is poor and they are living in a stable.'

He visited Bird in his tree. 'Welcoming party for the new baby in the stable,' he called. 'Hop along to the stable,' he bellowed to Rabbit.

The night was silent as the animals walked, hopped and flew to the stable. And sure enough there was the baby Jesus, with Mary his mother and Joseph.

Suddenly the silence was shattered
by the Animal Choir.

Come and sing to the new-born king,
the birds in the air, the fox in its lair,
things that creep or swim in the deep,
all creatures, praise the Lord.

Then each animal sang a solo. Ox was first.

I'm the Ox, I stand by the stall,
where lies the maker of us all.

Ass pricked up his ears.
I'm an Ass, that's what they say,
but I see Jesus born today.

Mouse sang very quietly.

I'm a Mouse, so small and grey,
for me this is a happy day.

Just then the shepherds arrived from the hills and the Sheep broke into song.

We're the Sheep, we love to graze,
for Jesus we will sing and praise.

Chicken flew to the rafters, bowed her head, and clucked in a whisper.
I'm a Chicken, scratching around,
and I'll adore without a sound.

Cat had found herself a nice pile of straw and she sang very sweetly.

I'm a Cat, all soft with fur;
for Jesus I will purr and purr.

Then who do you think came hopping
in – late as usual?
I'm a Rabbit with big long ears;
for Jesus' sake I'll give three cheers.

At last it was Dog's turn to welcome Jesus and he wanted to do something spectacular.

I'm a Dog, I jump up high,
and praise the Lord of earth and sky.

Here come the three wise men on the Camels who burst into song.

We're the Camels, tall and strong
who brought the three wise men
along.

And then all the animals sang together.
Silently, without a fuss,
he came to earth as one of us.
May he bless and help us all,
everyone both great and small.

After all the noise and singing the animals were quiet, happy that Jesus, the Saviour, had come to earth as his Father had promised.

Palm Tree Colouring Books are drawn by
Arthur Baker

The other titles in the series are

Following a Star
Noah's Big Boat
Jonah and the Big Fish
The Lost Son
Jesus goes to a Wedding
God makes the World
Daniel and the Lions
The Good Samaritan
The Lost Sheep

ISBN 0 86209 876 9
Catalogue No. 1300009

KEVIN MAYHEW LTD
Rattlesden
Bury St Edmunds
Suffolk IP30 0SZ